LINE OF DUTY

SWAT TEAMS

ARMED AND READY

by Connie Colwell Miller

Reading Consultant
Barbara J. Fox
Reading Specialist
North Carolina State University

Content Consultant
Kenneth E. deGraffenreid
Professor of Intelligence Studies
Institute of World Politics
Washington, D.C.

Capstone

Mankato, Minnesota

Blazers are published by Capstone Press,
151 Good Counsel Drive, P.O. Box 669, Mankato, Minnesota 56002.
www.capstonepress.com

Library of Congress Cataloging-in-Publication Data
Miller, Connie Colwell, 1976–
   SWAT teams: armed and ready / by Connie Colwell Miller.
   p. cm. — (Blazers. Line of duty)
   Summary: "Describes SWAT teams, including what they are and what
these teams do" — Provided by publisher.
   Includes bibliographical references and index.
   ISBN-13: 978-1-4296-1276-0 (hardcover)
   ISBN-10: 1-4296-1276-2 (hardcover)
   1. Police — Special weapons and tactics units — Juvenile literature.
2. Police training — Juvenile literature. 3. Police — Equipment and supplies
— Juvenile literature. I. Title. II. Series.
HV8080.S64M55 2008
363.2'32 — dc22   2007024747

Editorial Credits
Jennifer Besel, editor; Bobbi J. Wyss, designer; Wanda Winch, photo researcher

Photo Credits
911 Pictures/Bruce Cotler, 4–5; Luis Santana, 14–15; R. Lawrence Porter, 20
AP Images/Chitose Suzuki, 17; Los Angeles Daily News/Gene Blevins, 16;
    Matt Houston, cover; Oshkosh Northwestern/Shu-Ling Zhou, 28–29
Getty Images Inc./David Wilson Burnham, 25; Joe Raedle, 19
SuperStock, Inc./Ron Brown, 6–7
Zuma Press/Contra Costa Times/Bob Larson, 12; Contra Costa Times/Mark
    DuFrene, 26–27; Dang Ngo, 8–9, 13; Dennis Oda, 23; Gary Kieffer,
    10–11; Jonathan Moffat, 24

1 2 3 4 5 6 13 12 11 10 09 08

TABLE OF CONTENTS

CALLING IN THE SWAT TEAM

A drug dealer hides in an empty house. A SWAT team moves in to catch him before he runs away.

A woman threatens to stab someone. A SWAT team member takes **aim** with a rifle. He'll shoot if he has to.

[**aim** — to point a weapon]

 SWAT stands for Special Weapons and Tactics.

An angry crowd **riots** in the street. The SWAT team is called in. The team will work to get the crowd under control.

[**riot** — to act in a violent way]

SWAT members wear gear called hard tac during riots. This gear protects members from things that might be thrown at them.

SWAT BASICS

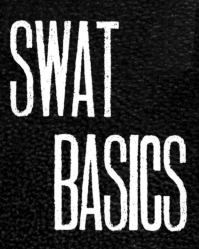

SWAT teams are part of local police forces. Team members are highly trained. They work to stop dangerous people from hurting others.

SWAT teams help the police
during risky missions. They help bring
murder **suspects** to jail. They are also
called in to control large crowds.

[**suspect** — someone thought to be guilty of a crime]

Some SWAT members are snipers. Snipers are very skilled at using guns. They can hit a target even from long distances.

Other SWAT members are trained to talk to dangerous criminals. They talk criminals out of hurting others.

SWAT members help people who have been harmed by a criminal.

WEAPONS AND EQUIPMENT

Team members often carry rifles or submachine guns. They use **tear gas** to stop some suspects.

[**tear gas** — a gas that causes a burning feeling in the eyes and lungs]

SWAT members wear body **armor** to protect their chests from bullets. They also wear helmets and face masks during the most dangerous jobs.

[**armor** — protective covering]

FACT! Members sometimes carry heavy shields to protect themselves from bullets.

Team members also wear vests with many pockets. Members carry a radio, handcuffs, and extra bullets in the pockets.

FACT! SWAT teams use round metal logs called rams to break down doors.

23

FACT!

Teams sometimes use thermal imaging. This equipment senses body heat, so teams can find criminals in the dark.

LOS ANGELES POLICE DEPARTME

SPECIAL WEAPONS AND TACTICS

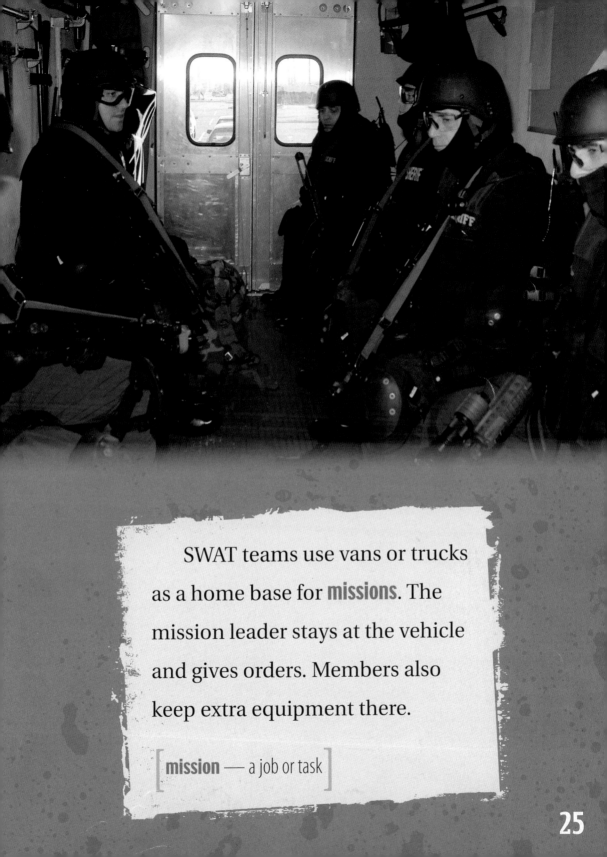

SWAT teams use vans or trucks as a home base for **missions**. The mission leader stays at the vehicle and gives orders. Members also keep extra equipment there.

[**mission** — a job or task]

STOPPING CRIMINALS

SWAT teams work to stop criminals from hurting others. Teams **arrest** gang members and drug dealers.

[**arrest** — to capture and hold someone for breaking the law]

SWAT members move slowly and carefully toward a criminal.

Every day, SWAT teams stop dangerous people. Members risk their lives to keep us safe.

GLOSSARY

aim (AYM) — pointing something in a particular direction

armor (AR-mur) — protective covering

arrest (uh-REST) — to capture and hold someone for breaking the law

mission (MISH-uhn) — a planned job or task

riot (RYE-uht) — to act in a violent and often uncontrollable way

suspect (SUHSS-pekt) — a person believed to be responsible for a crime

tear gas (TIHR GASS) — a gas that causes a burning feeling in the eyes and lungs

READ MORE

Gonzalez, Lissette. *Police in Action.* Dangerous Jobs. New York: PowerKids Press, 2008.

Goranson, Christopher D. *Police SWAT Teams: Life on High Alert.* Extreme Careers. New York: Rosen, 2003.

INTERNET SITES

FactHound offers a safe, fun way to find Internet sites related to this book. All of the sites on FactHound have been researched by our staff.

Here's how:
1. Visit *www.facthound.com*
2. Choose your grade level.
3. Type in this book ID **1429612762** for age-appropriate sites. You may also browse subjects by clicking on letters, or by clicking on pictures and words.
4. Click on the **Fetch It** button.

FactHound will fetch the best sites for you!

INDEX